# Embrace Your Worthiness

### Unlock Your True Potential and Conquer Self-Doubt for Lasting Success.

**Sherrie Salls**

## Copyright © 2024 [Sherrie R. Salls]

All rights reserved. No part of this publication may be reproduced, distributed, or transmitted in any form or by any means, including photocopying, recording, or other electronic or mechanical methods, without the prior written permission of the publisher, except in the case of brief quotations embodied in critical reviews and certain other noncommercial uses permitted by copyright law

## Disclaimer

The information provided in this book is for general purposes only. While every effort has been made to ensure the accuracy and completeness of the content, the author makes no representations or warranties, express or implied, regarding the suitability, applicability, or completeness of the information provided.

# Table of Contents

**Introduction:** ...................................................... 5
    Embracing Your Journey to Self-Worth .................. 5

**Part I:** ................................................................ 11
    1. Recognizing the Impact of Self-Doubt in Your Life ................................................................. 11
    2. Understanding Imposter Syndrome and Overcoming Self-Doubt ........................................ 17
    3. Breaking Free from Fear: ................................... 23

**Part II: Building Unshakable Self-Love** ........... 29
    4. Nurturing self love: ........................................... 37
    5. Celebrating Your Unique Worth: Embracing Your Authenticity ................................................. 43
    6. Healing and Restoring Confidence: Letting Go of Past Mistakes .................................................. 49

**Part III:** ............................................................. 55
**Unlearning Limiting Beliefs** ........................... 55
    7. Challenging Limiting Beliefs: Uncovering the Lies Holding You Back ................................................. 55
    8. Embodying Empowering Beliefs: Cultivating a Positive Mindset for Success .................................. 61
    9. Redefining Your Identity: Transforming Your Story and Perspective .............................................. 67

**Part IV: Embracing Your True Self** ................. 73
    10. Owning Your Worthiness: Embracing and Embodying Your Greatness .................................. 73

11. Living Authentically: Aligning Your Actions with Your Core Values ......................................................... 79
12. Nurturing Self-Care and Well-being: Prioritizing Your Worthiness and Well-being ............................. 85

**Part V: Manifesting Your Dreams** .................... 91

13. Setting Powerful Intentions: Clarifying Your Goals and Desires ......................................................... 91
14. Overcoming Obstacles: Building Resilience and Perseverance ............................................................... 97
15. Achieving True Fulfillment: Taking Aligned Action and Living with Purpose ............................ 103

**Conclusion:** ..................................................... 109
Embodying Your Worthiness Transformation ...... 109
**Review** ............................................................. 113

*"In the silence of self-belief, you'll find the loudest echoes of success."*

# Introduction:

## Embracing Your Journey to Self-Worth

Welcome to "Embrace Your Worthiness: How to Believe You Are Enough and Transform Your Life." This book is your guide, your companion, and your source of inspiration as you embark on a transformative journey towards embracing your true worth and unleashing your full potential.

In a world that often tells us we need to be more, do more, and achieve more to feel worthy, it's easy to lose sight of our inherent value. We find ourselves trapped in the cycle of self-doubt, questioning our abilities, and comparing ourselves to others. This constant striving for external validation can leave us feeling exhausted, unfulfilled, and disconnected from our true selves.

But here's the truth: You are already worthy, just as you are. You don't need to prove yourself to anyone or meet some arbitrary standard to be deserving of love, success, and happiness. Embracing your worthiness is about recognizing and embracing the unique essence that resides within you, and understanding that you are enough, exactly as you are.

This journey towards self-worth is not always easy. It requires courage, vulnerability, and a deep commitment to your own growth. It involves unlearning the limiting beliefs that have held you back, shedding the layers of self-doubt, and rediscovering the authentic, empowered version of yourself that has been waiting to emerge.

In this book, we will explore the multifaceted aspects of self-worth and provide you with practical tools, insights, and exercises to support your journey. We will delve into the impact of self-doubt on your life, relationships, and aspirations. We will uncover the lies that have kept you playing small and guide you in embracing empowering beliefs that will elevate your self-perception.

You will learn how to cultivate unshakable self-love, nurturing a compassionate and accepting relationship with yourself. By embracing your unique worth, you will discover the freedom to express your authenticity, unapologetically embracing your strengths, talents, and quirks. We will delve into the power of releasing past mistakes and restoring your self-confidence, allowing you to move forward with renewed purpose and conviction.

Throughout this journey, you will be encouraged to challenge the self-imposed limitations that have held you back. We will explore the transformative potential of rewriting your story, reframing your identity, and shifting your perspective. By doing so, you will gain a deeper understanding of who you truly are and the incredible potential that resides within you.

Embracing your worthiness is not an isolated act but a holistic approach to living. It involves nurturing your physical, emotional, and mental well-being. We will guide you in prioritizing self-care and developing practices that support your overall worthiness. By taking care of yourself, you will cultivate the resilience and strength needed to overcome obstacles and persevere on your path.

Ultimately, this book is an invitation to step into your greatness, to recognize your worthiness, and to live a life aligned with your deepest desires. It is a call to embrace your true self, to trust in your abilities, and to believe that you have what it takes to create the life you envision.

As you embark on this journey, remember that it is unique to you. Your path to self-worth may look different from others, and that is perfectly okay. Embrace your individuality, honor your progress, and be gentle with yourself along the way.

So, are you ready to embark on this transformative journey of self-discovery and self-acceptance? Are you ready to embrace your worthiness and step into the life you deserve? Let's begin this incredible adventure together and unlock the extraordinary potential that lies within you.

"Embrace your worthiness like the sun embraces the sky-boldly, unapologetically, and with endless warmth."

# Part I:

## 1. Recognizing the Impact of Self-Doubt in Your Life

Recognizing the cost of self-doubt in your life is an important aspect of understanding the impact it has on your overall well-being and self-worth. By acknowledging the negative consequences of self-doubt, you can cultivate a stronger motivation to overcome it and create affirmations that counteract its effects. Here are some key points to consider when reflecting on the cost of self-doubt:

*1. Impacts on Mental Health:* **Self-doubt** can significantly affect your mental health and emotional well-being. Constantly questioning your abilities, worth, and decisions can lead to anxiety, stress, and even depression. It can create a negative internal dialogue that undermines your confidence and prevents you from fully embracing your potential.

*2. Limiting Beliefs and Self-Limiting Behaviors:* Self-doubt often stems from deep-rooted limiting beliefs about yourself, such as "I'm not smart enough," "I don't deserve success," or "I always fail." These beliefs can hold you back from pursuing your goals, taking risks, and seizing opportunities. Self-doubt can create a cycle of self-sabotage, where you avoid challenges or settle for less than you deserve due to fear of failure or rejection.

*3. Strained Relationships:* Self-doubt can impact your relationships with others. It may lead to difficulties in establishing and maintaining healthy boundaries, as you may doubt your own worthiness of respect and love. Additionally, self-doubt can hinder your ability to express your needs, opinions, and emotions authentically, resulting in strained communication and a diminished sense of connection.

*4. Missed Opportunities for Growth:* **When self-doubt takes hold, you may hesitate to pursue opportunities that could lead to personal and professional growth. Fear of failure or judgment can prevent you from stepping outside of your comfort zone, trying new things, and embracing challenges. As a result, you may miss out on valuable experiences, learning opportunities, and the chance to discover your true potential.**

*5. Lowered Self-Esteem and Self-Worth:*

Self-doubt erodes self-esteem and self-worth over time. Constantly questioning your abilities and worthiness can create a negative self-perception, leading to feelings of inadequacy and unworthiness. This, in turn, can impact your confidence, decision-making, and overall sense of fulfillment and happiness.

*6. Impact on Well-Being and Quality of Life:* **Self-doubt can have a profound impact on your overall well-being and quality of life. It can contribute to increased stress levels, decreased resilience, and a diminished sense of self-care. Chronic self-doubt may also lead to physical symptoms such as fatigue, sleep disturbances, and compromised immune function.**

By recognizing the cost of self-doubt in your life, you gain a clearer understanding of its negative influence and the importance of actively working towards self-belief and self-worth. This awareness provides a strong motivation to challenge self-doubt and cultivate affirmations that counteract its effects. As you create your personalized list of affirmations, remember to focus on building self-confidence, embracing your worthiness, and nurturing a positive and empowering mindset that supports your growth and well-being.

"Though doubt may come knocking, your belief is what lets greatness in.

## 2. Understanding Imposter Syndrome and Overcoming Self-Doubt

Understanding Imposter Syndrome and overcoming self-doubt are crucial steps in cultivating a strong sense of self-worth and embracing your true capabilities. Here is an expanded exploration of these topics:

*1. Understanding Imposter Syndrome:*

**a. Definition**: Imposter Syndrome refers to the persistent feeling of being a fraud or fearing that your achievements are the result of luck rather than your abilities. It is characterized by an internal belief that you do not deserve your success and that others will eventually uncover your perceived incompetence.

b. *Common Signs and Manifestations*: Imposter Syndrome can manifest in various ways, including self-doubt, fear of failure, perfectionism, overworking, seeking constant validation, and downplaying achievements. It often affects high achievers who have difficulty internalizing their accomplishments.

c. *Causes and Contributing Factors*: Imposter Syndrome can stem from a combination of factors, such as perfectionism, early experiences of criticism or high expectations, societal pressures, and a lack of self-confidence. Cultural and gender norms can also play a role in exacerbating feelings of inadequacy.

d. *Impact on Self-Worth and Well-Being:* Imposter Syndrome can significantly impact self-worth and well-being. It can lead to chronic stress, anxiety, burnout, and a persistent sense of inadequacy. It may also hinder personal and professional growth, as individuals may avoid taking risks or pursuing opportunities due to fear of failure or being exposed as an imposter.

2. *Overcoming Self-Doubt*:

a. *Cultivating Self-Awareness:* Developing self-awareness is crucial in overcoming self-doubt. Start by recognizing and acknowledging your self-doubt triggers, patterns, and negative self-talk. By understanding the root causes of your self-doubt, you can begin to challenge and reframe those beliefs.

b. *Challenging Limiting Beliefs*: Actively challenge the negative beliefs that contribute to self-doubt. Question the evidence supporting these beliefs and seek counterexamples that demonstrate your competence and accomplishments. Practice replacing self-limiting thoughts with positive and affirming statements.

*c. Embracing Failure and Learning Opportunities:* Shift your perspective on failure and view it as an opportunity for growth and learning. Understand that setbacks and mistakes are natural parts of the learning process and do not define your worth or abilities. Embrace the lessons learned from failures and use them to propel yourself forward.

*d. Celebrating Achievements:* Take time to celebrate your achievements, no matter how small they may seem. Acknowledge your progress, strengths, and the effort you have put into your endeavors. Celebrating achievements helps build self-confidence and reinforces a positive self-image.

*e. Seeking Support and Building a Supportive Network:* Reach out to trusted friends, family, or mentors who can provide encouragement and support. Surround yourself with individuals who believe in your abilities and can offer constructive feedback. Additionally, consider seeking professional support through therapy or coaching to address deeper self-doubt issues.

*f. Practicing Self-Compassion:* Cultivate self-compassion by treating yourself with kindness and understanding. Be gentle with yourself when facing setbacks or challenges. Practice self-care, prioritize your well-being, and engage in activities that nourish your mind, body, and soul.

*g. Setting Realistic Goals and Taking* Action: Break down your goals into smaller, achievable steps. Setting realistic goals and taking action towards them builds confidence and helps combat self-doubt. Celebrate each milestone along the way, reinforcing your belief in your abilities.

*h. Embracing Growth Mindset:* Adopt a growth mindset, understanding that abilities and skills can be developed through dedication, effort, and learning. Embrace challenges as opportunities for growth and view setbacks as temporary obstacles on your journey towards success.

Overcoming self-doubt and navigating Imposter Syndrome is an ongoing process that requires patience, self-reflection, and consistent effort. By implementing these strategies and actively challenging self-doubt, you can cultivate a stronger sense of self-worth, embrace your capabilities, and thrive in various aspects of your life.

## 3. Breaking Free from Fear:

Breaking free from fear involves conquering specific fears that hold us back from reaching our full potential. Two common fears that significantly impact our lives are the fear of failure and the fear of rejection. Here's an explanation of how to overcome these fears:

*1. Fear of Failure:*

*a. Understanding the Nature of Failure:* **Recognize** that failure is a natural and inevitable part of life. It is not a reflection of your worth or abilities but rather an opportunity for growth and learning. Embrace a mindset that views failure as a stepping stone to success.

*b. Reframing Failure:* **Challenge** negative beliefs and perceptions surrounding failure. Instead of seeing it as a personal setback or a permanent state, reframe failure as a temporary situation that provides valuable feedback and insights. Embrace the idea that failure is a necessary part of the journey towards success.

*c. Setting Realistic Expectations:* **Unrealistic expectations can intensify the fear of failure. Set realistic goals and break them down into manageable steps. Celebrate small victories along the way, reinforcing your confidence and building momentum.**

*d. Embracing a Growth Mindset:* **Cultivate a growth mindset, which believes that abilities and skills can be developed through effort and learning. Embrace challenges as opportunities for growth and view setbacks as temporary obstacles that can be overcome with perseverance and resilience.**

*e. Learning from Failure:* **Instead of dwelling on failure, focus on extracting lessons and insights from the experience. Analyze what went wrong, why it** happened, and how you can improve moving forward. Use failure as a catalyst for personal and professional growth.

*2. Fear of Rejection:*

*a. Recognizing the Fear:* **Acknowledge that the fear of rejection is a common emotion experienced by many individuals. Understand that rejection is not a reflection of your worth as a person but often a result of circumstances, preferences, or subjective opinions.**

*b. Reframing Rejection:* **Challenge the notion that rejection is a personal attack or a permanent judgment on your abilities. Reframe rejection as a redirection towards better opportunities or a mismatch of expectations rather than a reflection of your value.**

*c. Building Resilience:* **Develop emotional resilience by strengthening your self-esteem and** self-worth. Cultivate a strong sense of identity and purpose that is not solely dependent on external validation. Surround yourself with supportive individuals who appreciate and value you for who you are.

*d. Taking Action despite Fear*: **Fear of rejection can paralyze us from taking necessary actions. Push yourself to step outside your comfort zone and take calculated risks. Remember that every rejection brings you one step closer to finding the right opportunity or connection.**

*e. Seeking Perspective:* **Reach out for feedback and constructive criticism. Understand that rejection can provide valuable insights and opportunities for growth. Seek mentors or trusted individuals who can offer guidance and help you navigate through challenging situations.**

*f. Celebrating Resilience:* **Celebrate your resilience in the face of rejection. Recognize and appreciate the** courage it takes to put yourself out there and accept that not every venture will be successful. By celebrating your efforts and perseverance, you reinforce a positive mindset that helps you overcome future rejections.

Breaking free from the fear of failure and rejection requires self-awareness, self-compassion, and a willingness to challenge negative beliefs. By reframing these fears, adopting a growth mindset, and taking deliberate actions, you can gradually conquer these fears and unlock your true potential.

*Belief in oneself is the first step towards success."*

# Part II: Building Unshakable Self-Love

Building unshakable self-love is a transformative journey that involves cultivating a deep and unwavering sense of love, acceptance, and compassion towards oneself. It requires embracing your worthiness, celebrating your strengths, and embracing your imperfections. Here's an expanded explanation of how to build unshakable self-love,

*1.Self acceptance and self compassion*

*a. Recognizing Your Inherent Worth:* **Understand** that your worth as a human being is not contingent upon external achievements, appearances, or opinions of others. You are inherently valuable and deserving of love and respect simply because you exist.

*b. Embracing Imperfections*: **Embrace your imperfections as part of what makes you unique and human. Accept that making mistakes or having flaws does not diminish your worth. Treat yourself with kindness, understanding, and forgiveness.**

*c. Cultivating Self-Compassion:* **Extend compassion to yourself in moments of struggle or self-doubt. Practice self-care, engage in activities that nourish your soul, and prioritize your well-being. Treat yourself as you would treat a dear friend, offering support and understanding.**

Imagine a young woman named Maya who had always struggled with accepting her physical appearance. She constantly compared herself to unrealistic beauty standards, leading to a deep sense of self-doubt and insecurity. One day, Maya came across a book that emphasized the importance of self-love and acceptance. Inspired, she decided to embark on a journey of self-discovery and self-compassion. Maya started practicing daily affirmations, reminding herself of her unique beauty and worth. She also sought out positive role models who celebrated diverse body types and embraced their own imperfections. Over time, Maya's self-love blossomed, and she learned to appreciate herself just as she was, radiating confidence and inspiring others to do the same.

*2. Celebrating Your Strengths and Accomplishments:*

*a. Identifying Your Strengths:* **Take inventory of your strengths, talents, and positive qualities. Recognize the unique gifts and abilities that you bring to the world. Celebrate your achievements, no matter how small they may seem.**

*b. Gratitude and Self-Appreciation:* **Practice gratitude for the person you are and the progress you** have made. Take moments to appreciate and acknowledge your efforts and accomplishments. Develop a habit of regularly expressing gratitude for yourself.

*c. Setting Healthy Boundaries:* **Establish** and maintain boundaries that honor your self-worth and protect your emotional well-being. Learn to say no to activities or relationships that deplete your energy or compromise your values. Prioritize self-care and honor your needs.

Meet Alex, a young professional who struggled with acknowledging his accomplishments. Despite receiving praise from colleagues and clients, Alex always downplayed his achievements and attributed them to luck or external factors. One day, a close friend encouraged him to start a gratitude journal. Alex began jotting down three things he appreciated about himself each day, including his talents, skills, and personal qualities. As he reflected on his entries over time, Alex realized the depth of his strengths and the impact he had on others. This newfound appreciation for himself propelled him to pursue new opportunities and embrace his abilities with confidence.

*3. Embracing Self-Care and Personal Growth:*

*a. Prioritizing Self-Care:* Make self-care a non-negotiable part of your routine. Engage in activities that bring you joy, relaxation, and fulfillment. Nurture your physical, emotional, and mental well-being.

*b. Continuous Learning and Personal Growth:* Embrace lifelong learning and personal growth. Set goals that challenge you and align with your values. Celebrate the progress you make along the way, recognizing that growth and development are ongoing processes.

*c. Surrounding Yourself with Supportive Relationships:* Surround yourself with individuals who uplift and support you. Cultivate meaningful relationships that encourage your growth and celebrate your journey towards self-love. Seek out mentors, friends, or support groups that foster positivity and acceptance.

Sarah, a busy professional and mother, had always struggled with prioritizing her own needs. She constantly put others before herself, leading to burnout and neglect of her own well-being. One day, Sarah realized that she needed to make self-care a priority. She started setting aside time each day for activities that brought her joy and relaxation, such as reading, practicing yoga, and spending time in nature.

Additionally, she joined a supportive community of like-minded individuals who shared her commitment to self-care and personal growth. Sarah's journey towards unshakable self-love not only transformed her own life but also inspired those around her to prioritize their well-being.

Building unshakable self-love is a lifelong journey that requires self-reflection, self-compassion, and intentional actions. By embracing self-acceptance, celebrating your strengths, nurturing personal growth, and surrounding yourself with positivity, you can cultivate a deep sense of love and acceptance for yourself that transcends external circumstances and empowers you to live a fulfilling and authentic life.

*Your potential knows no bounds; it's your self-doubt that draws the lines."*

## 4. Nurturing self love:

Nurturing self-love involves developing and maintaining a positive, compassionate, and supportive relationship with yourself. It requires prioritizing your well-being, practicing self-care, and fostering a deep sense of self-acceptance and self-worth. Here's an expanded explanation of how to cultivate a positive relationship with yourself:

*1. Prioritizing Self-Care:*

*a. Physical Self-Care:* **Take** care of your physical health by nourishing your body with nutritious food, engaging in regular exercise, and getting enough restful sleep. Listen to your body's needs and honor them.

*b. Emotional Self-Care:* **Pay** attention to your emotional well-being. Engage in activities that bring you joy, such as hobbies, spending time with loved ones, or practicing mindfulness and meditation.

Allow yourself to feel and process your emotions without judgment.

*c. Mental Self-Care:* **Take** care of your mental health by engaging in activities that stimulate your mind, such as reading, learning, or engaging in creative pursuits. Practice self-compassion and challenge negative self-talk or limiting beliefs.

*d. Spiritual Self-Care:* **Nurture your spiritual well-being in a way that resonates with you. This can include practicing gratitude, engaging in meaningful rituals or practices, or connecting with nature or a higher power.**

*2. Cultivating Self-Acceptance:*

*a. Embracing Your Uniqueness:* **Celebrate** your individuality and embrace your strengths, quirks, and imperfections. Recognize that no one is perfect, and that your unique qualities contribute to your identity and value.

*b. Practicing Self-Compassion:* **Treat yourself with** kindness and understanding, especially during times of difficulty or failure. Offer yourself the same compassion and support you would give to a loved one. Embrace self-forgiveness and let go of self-blame.

*c. Letting Go of Comparison:* **Avoid** comparing yourself to others, as it can lead to feelings of inadequacy and self-doubt. Focus on your own journey, progress, and growth. Celebrate your accomplishments without diminishing them in comparison to others.

*d. Setting Healthy Boundaries:* **Establish** and maintain boundaries that honor your needs, values, and well-being. Learn to say no to situations or relationships that drain your energy or compromise your self-respect.

*3. Developing Self-Worth:*

*a. Acknowledging Your Value*: **Recognize that you are worthy of love, respect, and happiness simply because you exist. Your worth is not contingent upon external achievements, validation, or the opinions of others.**

*b. Celebrating Your Achievements:* **Acknowledge and celebrate your accomplishments, no matter how big or small. Take time to reflect on your progress and growth. Develop a practice of regularly acknowledging and appreciating your achievements.**

*c. Affirming Self-Positive Beliefs:* **Challenge negative self-beliefs and replace them with positive affirmations. Focus on your strengths, capabilities, and potential. Surround yourself with positive influences that reinforce your self-worth.**

*d. Seeking Support:* **Reach out to trusted friends, family members, or professionals who can provide support and guidance on your journey towards self-**

love. Consider working with a therapist or coach who can help you navigate any challenges or barriers you may encounter.

Expanding on the topic, let's consider the story of Emma. Emma had always struggled with low self-esteem and self-doubt. She constantly sought validation from others, seeking their approval to feel worthy and lovable.

However, one day, Emma realized that she had been neglecting her own needs and happiness in the process. Determined to cultivate a positive relationship with herself, Emma embarked on a journey of self-discovery and self-love. She began by prioritizing self-care, engaging in activities that brought her joy and fulfillment.

Emma also practiced self-compassion, treating herself with kindness and understanding during moments of challenge or failure. She let go of comparing herself to others and focused on her own progress and growth. With time, Emma developed a deep sense of self-acceptance and self-worth.

She celebrated her achievements, acknowledged her strengths, and embraced her uniqueness. Emma's newfound self-love radiated in her relationships and her overall well-being, inspiring those around her to embark on their own journeys of self-discovery and self-love.

Nurturing self-love is an ongoing process that requires self-awareness, self-compassion, and intentional actions. By prioritizing self-care, cultivating self-acceptance, and developing a strong sense of self-worth, you can build a positive and empowering relationship with yourself that enhances your overall happiness and well-being.

## 5. Celebrating Your Unique Worth: Embracing Your Authenticity

Celebrating your unique worth and embracing your authenticity is a powerful way to cultivate self-love and strengthen your relationship with yourself. It involves recognizing and honoring your true self, letting go of societal expectations, and embracing the beauty of being authentically and unapologetically you. Here's an expanded explanation of how to embrace your authenticity and celebrate your unique worth:

*1. Self Reflection and Self Discovery*

*a. Explore Your Values and Passions:* **Take** time to reflect on what truly matters to you and what brings you joy and fulfillment. Identify your core values and align your life with them. Engage in activities that ignite your passions and bring out your authentic self.

*b. Uncover Your Strengths and Talents:* **Reflect** on your unique strengths, talents, and skills. Recognize the qualities that set you apart and make you special. Embrace these strengths and find ways to express and share them with the world.

*c. Embrace Your Story:* **Your** life experiences, both positive and challenging, have shaped you into the person you are today. Embrace your story, including the lessons learned and the wisdom gained. Recognize that your journey is a valuable part of your authenticity.

*2. Letting Go of Societal Expectations:*

*a. Challenge Unrealistic Standards:* **Society** often imposes unrealistic standards of beauty, success, and happiness. Recognize that these standards are arbitrary and subjective. Reject the pressure to conform and instead define success and happiness on your own terms.

*b. Embrace Your Uniqueness:* **Embrace the qualities that make you different from others. Celebrate your quirks, your individual style, and your unconventional choices. Remember that your uniqueness is what makes you stand out and contributes to the richness of the world.**

*c. Authentic Communication:* **Practice open and honest communication with yourself and others. Express your thoughts, feelings, and opinions authentically, without fear of judgment or rejection. Embrace vulnerability and allow yourself to be seen for who you truly are.**

*3. Cultivating Self-Acceptance:*

*a. Embrace Imperfection:* **Accept that no one is perfect, including yourself. Embrace your flaws and** imperfections as part of your authentic self. Understand that making mistakes and experiencing setbacks are essential for growth and learning.

*b. Practice Self-Compassion:* **Treat** yourself with kindness and compassion, especially during challenging times. Offer yourself the same understanding and support you would give to a loved one. Embrace self-forgiveness and let go of self-criticism.

*c. Surround Yourself With Accepting Relationships:* Seek out relationships and communities that accept and celebrate your authentic self. Surround yourself with people who appreciate and value you for who you are. Let go of toxic relationships that do not support your authenticity.

Meet James, a young professional who had always felt pressured to conform to societal expectations. He realized that he was living a life that didn't align with his values and passions. James decided to embark on a journey of self-discovery and authenticity. He took time to reflect on his true desires and interests. James courageously pursued his passion for art, even though it was considered unconventional by societal standards. He embraced his unique artistic style and expressed his creativity authentically. As James started living in alignment with his authentic self, he found a sense of fulfillment and happiness that he had never experienced before. His authentic expression inspired others to embrace their own uniqueness and pursue their passions fearlessly.

Embracing your authenticity and celebrating your unique worth is a liberating and empowering process. By reflecting on your values, letting go of societal expectations, and cultivating self-acceptance, you can embrace your true self and live a life that is authentic and fulfilling. Remember, celebrating your unique worth is not only a gift to yourself but also an invitation for others to do the same.

# 6. Healing and Restoring Confidence: Letting Go of Past Mistakes

Healing and restoring confidence involves the process of letting go of past mistakes and embracing self-forgiveness. It requires acknowledging that everyone makes mistakes and recognizing that those mistakes do not define your worth or future potential. Here's an expanded explanation on how to let go of past mistakes and regain confidence:

*1. Acceptance and Self-Compassion:*

*a. Acknowledge Your Mistakes*: **Recognize and accept the mistakes you've made in the past. Avoid denying or suppressing them, as this can hinder your ability to heal and move forward.**

*b. Practice Self-Compassion:* **Treat yourself with kindness and understanding. Understand that making mistakes is a part of being human and that everyone experiences setbacks and failures at some point. Offer yourself the same empathy and support you would give to a friend in a similar situation.**

*c. Learn from Mistakes*: **Reflect on the lessons and growth opportunities that come from your mistakes. Instead of dwelling on the negative aspects, focus on the valuable insights and knowledge you've gained. Use these lessons to make better choices in the future.**

## 2. Release Guilt and Shame:

*a. Challenge Negative Self-Talk:* **Be aware of any negative self-talk or self-blame related to your past mistakes. Replace these thoughts with more compassionate and realistic perspectives. Remind yourself that you are human and deserving of forgiveness.**

*b. Practice Forgiveness:* **Forgive yourself for the mistakes you've made. Holding onto guilt and shame only prolongs your suffering and prevents you from moving forward. Embrace the opportunity to grow, learn, and become a better version of yourself.**

*c. Seek Support:* **Share your feelings with trusted friends, family, or professionals who can provide support and perspective. Sometimes, talking about your experiences with others can help alleviate guilt and shame and provide a fresh outlook.**

*3. Focus on Personal Growth:*

*a. Set Realistic Expectations:* **Understand that personal growth is a continuous journey, and it takes time. Set realistic expectations for yourself and be patient as you work towards rebuilding your confidence.**

*b. Celebrate Progress:* **Acknowledge** and celebrate your achievements, no matter how small they may seem. Recognize the efforts you've made to learn from your mistakes and make positive changes in your life.

*c. Embrace Self-Development:* **Engage** in activities that promote personal growth and self-improvement. This can include reading books, attending workshops or courses, seeking therapy or counseling, or practicing mindfulness and self-reflection.

Let's consider the journey of Sarah, who had made a significant mistake in her professional life that affected her self-confidence. Initially, she struggled with feelings of guilt and shame, which held her back from moving forward.

However, Sarah decided to confront her past mistakes and embarked on a healing journey. Through self-compassion and self-forgiveness, she gradually released the burden of guilt and shame. Sarah focused on personal growth, seeking support from mentors and attending professional development programs. Over time, she regained her confidence and started embracing new opportunities. Sarah's story is a testament to the power of letting go of past mistakes and reclaiming self-assurance.

Letting go of past mistakes is essential for healing and restoring confidence. By practicing self-compassion, releasing guilt and shame, and focusing on personal growth, you can move forward with a renewed sense of self-worth and confidence. Remember, your past does not define your future, and every mistake is an opportunity for growth and self-improvement.

*Like a seed reaching for the sun, your worthiness grows with each step towards the light."*

# Part III:

# Unlearning Limiting Beliefs

## 7. Challenging Limiting Beliefs: Uncovering the Lies Holding You Back

*1. Recognizing Limiting Beliefs:*

*a. Self-Reflection:* **Take** time to reflect on your thoughts, attitudes, and beliefs about yourself and the world around you. Identify any recurring patterns of negative or self-limiting beliefs that may be holding you back.

*b. Awareness of Conditioning:* **Understand** that many of our beliefs are shaped by our upbringing, societal influences, and past experiences. Recognize that these beliefs may not always reflect reality and can limit your potential.

*c. Identifying Specific Limiting Beliefs:* **Pinpoint** the specific beliefs that are holding you back. These beliefs often manifest as self-doubt, fear, or feelings of inadequacy. Examples include beliefs such as "I'm not smart enough," "I don't deserve success," or "I will never be able to achieve my goals."

*2. Challenging and Examining Beliefs:*

*a. Gather Evidence:* **Challenge** your limiting beliefs by seeking evidence that contradicts them. Look for examples of people who have overcome similar challenges or achieved what you aspire to achieve. This can help you see that your beliefs are not absolute truths.

*b. Question Assumptions:* **Ask yourself critical questions to examine the validity of your beliefs. What evidence supports these beliefs? Are there alternative perspectives or explanations? Are the beliefs based on facts or assumptions?**

*c. Reframing Beliefs:* **Replace limiting beliefs with empowering and supportive ones. Focus on affirmations that reinforce your strengths, potential, and resilience. For example, replace "I'm not good enough" with "I have unique talents and abilities that contribute value."**

*3. Cultivating Empowering Beliefs:*

*a. Visualization and Affirmations:* **Use visualization techniques to imagine yourself succeeding and overcoming challenges. Repeat positive affirmations that counteract your limiting beliefs. Visualizing and affirming your success can gradually rewire your subconscious mind.**

b. *Surround Yourself With Supportive Influences:* Seek out positive and supportive environments, communities, and individuals who uplift and inspire you. Surround yourself with people who believe in your potential and encourage your growth.

c. *Take Action:* Challenge your limiting beliefs by taking small steps outside your comfort zone. Each success will reinforce your new empowering beliefs and expand your confidence.

Let's consider the story of Alex, who held a limiting belief that they were not creative enough to pursue their passion for painting. Alex constantly compared themselves to other artists and doubted their own artistic abilities.

However, Alex decided to challenge this belief by seeking evidence of successful artists who started with minimal skills. They also joined a supportive art community that encouraged experimentation and growth. Through persistent practice and reframing their belief, Alex gradually embraced their creativity and developed their unique artistic style.

Alex's story demonstrates the transformative power of challenging limiting beliefs and the importance of surrounding oneself with supportive influences.

By recognizing and challenging limiting beliefs, you can uncover the lies that hold you back and replace them with empowering beliefs that support your growth and success. Through self-reflection, critical examination, and cultivating empowering beliefs, you can break free from the constraints of self-doubt and unlock your true potential. Remember, your beliefs shape your reality, so choose beliefs that empower and inspire you to reach new heights.

"Embrace your worthiness like the sun embraces the sky-boldly, unapologetically, and with endless warmth."

# 8. Embodying Empowering Beliefs: Cultivating a Positive Mindset for Success

Embodying Empowering Beliefs: Cultivating a Positive Mindset for Success

*1. Understanding the Power of Beliefs:*

*a. Beliefs and Mindset:* **Recognize** that your beliefs shape your thoughts, emotions, and actions. Empowering beliefs have the potential to fuel your motivation, resilience, and success.

*b. Identifying Empowering Beliefs:* **Reflect** on the beliefs that align with your goals and values. These may include beliefs such as "I have the ability to learn and grow," "Challenges are opportunities for growth," or "I am deserving of success."

*c. Embracing Growth Mindset:* **Adopt a growth mindset, which is the belief that abilities and intelligence can be developed through effort, learning, and perseverance. Embrace challenges, view failures as learning opportunities, and maintain a focus on continuous improvement.**

*2. Cultivating a Positive Mindset:*

*a. Self-Awareness:* **Pay attention to your thoughts and self-talk. Notice any negative or self-limiting patterns and consciously replace them with positive and empowering thoughts.**

*b. Gratitude and Appreciation:* **Practice gratitude by acknowledging and appreciating the positive aspects of your life. This mindset shift towards gratitude can enhance positivity and resilience.**

*c. Positive Affirmations:* **Use positive affirmations to reinforce empowering beliefs. Repeat statements such as "I am capable of achieving my goals," "I have** the resources to overcome challenges," or "I am deserving of success." Affirmations help rewire your subconscious mind and reinforce positive self-perception.

*3. Taking Action and Building Resilience:*

*a. Goal Setting:* Set clear, attainable goals that align with your values and aspirations. Break them down into actionable steps and celebrate milestones along the way. This provides a sense of progress and boosts motivation.

*b. Embracing Failure as Learning:* View failures as stepping stones to success. Instead of letting setbacks discourage you, analyze them as opportunities for growth and learning. Embrace a mindset of resilience and perseverance.

*c. Self-Care and Well-being:* Prioritize self-care activities that nurture your physical, emotional, and mental well-being. Engage in activities such as exercise, mindfulness, adequate sleep, and connecting with supportive relationships. A healthy mind and body contribute to a positive mindset.

Let's consider the story of Maya, who wanted to start her own business but held self-doubts and limiting beliefs about her abilities. Maya decided to embody empowering beliefs by shifting her mindset. She practiced gratitude, focusing on the positive aspects of her journey. Maya also utilized positive affirmations to reinforce her confidence and capability.

With each step she took towards her goals, Maya built resilience and embraced failures as learning opportunities. Through consistent action and a positive mindset, Maya successfully launched her business, proving to herself that embodying empowering beliefs is instrumental in achieving success.

By embodying empowering beliefs and cultivating a positive mindset, you can create a strong foundation for success. By recognizing the power of beliefs, developing a growth mindset, and fostering a positive outlook, you can overcome challenges, persist in the face of setbacks, and achieve your goals. Remember, your mindset shapes your reality, so choose beliefs that empower and inspire you to reach new heights.

*Your worthiness isn't measured by the applause of others, but by the quiet confidence within."*

# 9. Redefining Your Identity: Transforming Your Story and Perspective

***1. Reflecting on Your Current Identity:***

*a. Self-Reflection:* **Take time to reflect on how you currently perceive yourself and the story you tell about your life. Examine the beliefs, labels, and narratives that you have internalized and how they shape your identity.**

*b. Identifying Limiting Beliefs:* **Recognize any limiting beliefs or negative self-perceptions that hold you back and prevent you from fully embracing your true potential. These beliefs might include thoughts like "I'm not good enough" or "I always fail."**

*c. Celebrating Your Strengths and Accomplishments:* **Acknowledge your strengths,** talents, and past achievements. Reflect on the moments when you've overcome challenges and experienced success. Celebrating your accomplishments helps build a positive foundation for redefining your identity.

*2. Shifting Your Story and Perspective:*

a. Rewriting Your Narrative: **Challenge** and reframe the negative or limiting aspects of your story. Focus on the lessons learned, growth, and resilience you have demonstrated. Emphasize the positive aspects and potential for future success.

b. *Embracing Empowering Beliefs:* **Replace** self-limiting beliefs with empowering beliefs that reflect your true potential. Affirmations such as "I am capable of achieving my goals" or "I deserve happiness and success" can help reshape your perspective.

*c. Embracing Change and Adaptability:* **Recognize** that change is a natural part of life. Embrace the idea that your identity is not fixed; it can evolve and grow as you do. Embrace the opportunity to redefine yourself and explore new possibilities.

*3. Cultivating a Growth Mindset:*

*a. Embracing Challenges:* **View** challenges as opportunities for growth and learning. Embrace them with a mindset that focuses on the process rather than solely on the outcome. See setbacks as stepping stones toward success.

*b. Seeking Continuous Learning:* **Adopt** a mindset of curiosity and a desire for personal growth. Engage in activities that expand your knowledge, skills, and perspectives. This can include reading books, taking courses, seeking mentorship, or pursuing new hobbies.

*c. Surrounding Yourself with Support:* **Surround** yourself with individuals who uplift and support your growth. Seek out mentors, friends, or communities that inspire and encourage you to embrace your new identity and perspective.

Let's consider the story of James, who had always defined himself as shy and lacking confidence. However, James decided to redefine his identity and transform his story. He challenged the belief that he was shy by actively seeking opportunities to step out of his comfort zone.

James embraced empowering beliefs such as "I am capable of connecting with others" and "I possess the confidence to express myself." Through consistent efforts and a growth mindset, James gradually transformed his identity and gained confidence in social settings. James' story illustrates the power of redefining our identity and shifting our perspective to unlock our true potential.

By reflecting on your current identity, challenging limiting beliefs, and embracing empowering beliefs, you can redefine your story and transform your perspective. Cultivating a growth mindset, embracing change, and surrounding yourself with support contribute to your personal growth and self-discovery. Remember, you have the power to shape your identity and create a narrative that aligns with your aspirations and potential.

"You are the author of your story–fill each page with the ink of confidence and the pen of purpose."

# Part IV: Embracing Your True Self

## 10. Owning Your Worthiness: Embracing and Embodying Your Greatness

*1. Recognizing Your Inherent Worth:*

*a. Self-Acceptance:* **Embrace the understanding** that you are inherently worthy and deserving of love, success, and happiness. Recognize that your worth is not dependent on external factors such as achievements or validation from others.

*b. Letting Go of Comparison:* **Release** the habit of comparing yourself to others. Acknowledge that everyone has their unique journey and strengths. Focus on your own progress and growth instead of measuring yourself against others.

*c. Embracing Imperfections:* **Embrace** your imperfections and see them as part of what makes you unique. Understand that making mistakes and experiencing setbacks are natural parts of the growth process.

## 2. Embracing Your Greatness:

*a. Identifying Your Strengths and Talents:* **Reflect** on your strengths, talents, and qualities that set you apart. Acknowledge and appreciate the unique gifts and abilities you possess.

*b. Celebrating Achievements:* **Take** time to celebrate your accomplishments, both big and small. Recognize the effort and dedication you put into your successes. Celebrating achievements reinforces your belief in your own greatness.

*c. Positive Self-Talk:* **Cultivate a habit of positive self-talk and self-encouragement. Replace self-doubt and self-criticism with affirmations that reinforce your worthiness and greatness. Remind yourself of your capabilities and potential.**

*3. Embodying Your Greatness:*

*a. Stepping into Your Power:* **Take ownership of your worthiness by stepping into your personal power. Trust in yourself and your abilities. Make choices and decisions that align with your values and aspirations.**

*b. Setting Boundaries:* **Establish healthy boundaries that protect your time, energy, and well-being. Say no to activities or relationships that do not serve your growth and greatness. Prioritize self-care and prioritize activities that nourish your mind, body, and spirit.

*c. Taking Inspired Action*: Act on your dreams and aspirations. Break down your goals into actionable steps and take consistent, inspired action towards them. Each step forward reinforces your belief in your own greatness.

Let's consider the story of Sarah, who struggled with feelings of unworthiness and self-doubt. However, Sarah decided to own her worthiness and embrace her greatness. She started by acknowledging her strengths, talents, and past accomplishments.

Sarah practiced positive self-talk and replaced self-doubt with affirmations that affirmed her worthiness. As she began to embody her greatness, Sarah took bold steps towards her goals and dreams. She set boundaries in her personal and professional life, prioritizing her well-being and growth. Sarah's journey demonstrates the transformative power of owning one's worthiness and embracing personal greatness.

By recognizing your inherent worth, embracing your greatness, and embodying it in your daily life, you can live authentically and confidently. Embrace self-acceptance, let go of comparison, and celebrate your achievements. Step into your power, set boundaries, and take inspired action. Remember, you are worthy of all the love, success, and happiness life has to offer. Own your worthiness and embrace your greatness with conviction and authenticity.

*Embrace self-acceptance, let go of comparison, and celebrate your achievements.*

## 11. Living Authentically: Aligning Your Actions with Your Core Values

Living authentically means aligning your actions with your core values and being true to yourself. Here's an expanded version of the unit on living authentically:

*1. Understanding Core Values:*

  *a. Self-Reflection:* **Take** time to reflect on your core values—the principles and beliefs that are most important to you. Consider what truly matters to you in various areas of life, such as relationships, career, personal growth, and ethics.

  *b. Identifying Core Values*: Identify your core values by determining what brings you a sense of fulfillment, purpose, and alignment. Examples of core values include integrity, compassion, authenticity, growth, and balance.

*c. Prioritizing Values:* **Rank** your core values in order of importance. This exercise helps you gain clarity on what values you want to prioritize when making decisions and taking action.

*2. Aligning Actions with Core Values:*

*a. Values-Based Decision Making:* **Make** choices that align with your core values. When faced with a decision, consider how each option aligns with your values. Choose the path that resonates with your inner truth and supports your authenticity.

*b. Setting Goals in Alignment with Values:* **Set** meaningful goals that align with your core values. Ensure that your aspirations and actions are in harmony with what you hold dear. This alignment fosters a sense of purpose and fulfillment.

*c. Integrity and Authenticity:* **Be** true to yourself and maintain integrity by aligning your actions with your core values. Live and express your values authentically in your interactions, relationships, and work.

### 3. Overcoming Obstacles:

*a. Self-Awareness:* **Cultivate** self-awareness to recognize when your actions or choices are not in alignment with your values. Pay attention to any feelings of discomfort or inner conflict as indicators that adjustments may be necessary.

*b. Courage and Resilience:* **Embrace** the courage to make changes and take action in alignment with your values, even if it requires stepping out of your comfort zone. Develop resilience to overcome challenges and setbacks that may arise along the way.

*c. Practice Mindfulness:* **Cultivate** mindfulness to stay present and connected with your values in your daily life. Regularly check in with yourself to ensure that your actions and decisions reflect your authentic self.

Let's consider the story of Alex, who valued environmental sustainability. However, Alex realized that their actions were not aligned with this core value. They made a commitment to live authentically by aligning their actions with their values.

Alex started by making sustainable choices in their daily life, such as reducing waste and adopting eco-friendly practices. They also volunteered for environmental organizations, aligning their career with their values. Through consistent action and a commitment to living authentically, Alex found a deep sense of purpose and fulfillment.

Living authentically by aligning your actions with your core values allows you to live a more meaningful and fulfilling life. By reflecting on your values, making values-based decisions, and setting goals that align with your values, you ensure that your actions are in harmony with your authentic self. Overcoming obstacles requires self-awareness, courage, and resilience. Remember, living authentically is a lifelong journey of self-discovery and growth, allowing you to lead a life that is true to yourself

*"Raise your head, for you are planted in the soil of merit, doused with resilience's showers and fed by the sun of self-belief."*

## 12. Nurturing Self-Care and Well-being: Prioritizing Your Worthiness and Well-being

*1. Recognizing the Importance of Self-Care:*

*a. Understanding Self-Care:* **Self-care refers to intentional actions and practices that promote your physical, mental, and emotional well-being. It involves taking care of your needs and nurturing yourself on a regular basis.**

*b. Prioritizing Yourself:* **Recognize that self-care is not selfish; it is essential for your overall well-being. Understand that by prioritizing your own needs, you are better equipped to support and care for others.**

*c. Personalizing Self-Care:* **Explore and experiment with various self-care practices to find what resonates with you. Self-care is a highly individualized process, and what works for someone** else may not work for you. Find activities that bring you joy, relaxation, and rejuvenation.

## 2. Physical Self-Care:

*a. Prioritizing Sleep:* **Ensure** you get adequate sleep to support your physical and mental well-being. Establish a consistent sleep routine and create a sleep-friendly environment.

*b. Nourishing Nutrition:* **Pay** attention to your dietary habits and strive to consume a balanced and nutritious diet. Stay hydrated, incorporate fruits and vegetables, and limit the intake of processed foods.

*c. Regular Exercise:* **Engage** in regular physical activity that you enjoy. Find activities that promote movement and contribute to your overall fitness and vitality.

## 3. Emotional and Mental Self-Care:

*a. Emotional Awareness:* **Cultivate emotional intelligence and awareness of your feelings. Practice self-compassion and allow yourself to feel and process emotions without judgment.**

*b. Stress Management:* **Develop healthy coping mechanisms to manage stress effectively. This can include practices such as meditation, deep breathing exercises, journaling, or engaging in hobbies that bring you joy.**

*c. Mental Stimulation:* **Engage in activities that stimulate your mind, such as reading, puzzles, learning new skills, or engaging in creative pursuits. Continuously challenge yourself intellectually to foster growth and mental well-being.**

*4. Nurturing Relationships and Connection*

*a. Building Supportive Networks:* **Cultivate relationships with individuals who uplift and** support you. Surround yourself with people who appreciate and value you for who you are.

*b. Setting Boundaries:* **Establish boundaries in your relationships to protect your well-being. Learn to say no and prioritize your needs when necessary.**

*c. Meaningful Connections:* **Seek out and nurture meaningful connections with others. Engage in open and authentic communication that fosters understanding and connection.**

## 5. Cultivating Self-Compassion:

*a. Practicing Self-Kindness:* **Treat yourself with kindness and compassion. Practice positive self-talk and offer yourself the same support and understanding you would give to a loved one.**

*b. Embracing Imperfection:* **Accept that you are human and that making mistakes and experiencing** setbacks is a natural part of life. Embrace self-forgiveness and learn from challenges and failures.

*c. Prioritizing Rest and Leisure:* **Allow yourself to rest and engage in activities that bring you joy and relaxation. Set aside time for leisure and hobbies that recharge and rejuvenate you.**

Let's consider the story of Maya, who struggled with burnout and neglecting her well-being. However, Maya decided to prioritize self-care and well-being. She established a daily self-care routine that included meditation, regular exercise, and spending quality time with loved ones.

Maya also learned to set boundaries in her personal and professional life, allowing her to prioritize her own needs. Through consistent self-care practices, Maya experienced increased energy, improved mental well-being, and a greater sense of worthiness.

Nurturing self-care and well-being is essential for your overall health and worthiness. Prioritize physical self-care, emotional and mental well-being, and nurturing relationships. Cultivate self-compassion and practice setting boundaries. Remember, self-care is not a luxury but a necessity. By prioritizing your well-being, you honor your worthiness and create a foundation for a fulfilling and balanced life.

# Part V: Manifesting Your Dreams

## 13. Setting Powerful Intentions: Clarifying Your Goals and Desires

*1. Reflecting on Your Desires:*

*a. Self-Reflection:* Take time to reflect on your desires and aspirations. Consider what you truly want in different areas of your life, such as career, relationships, personal growth, health, and well-being.

*b. Identifying Values:* Align your goals and desires with your core values. Ensure that they are in harmony with what you hold dear and what brings you a sense of fulfillment and purpose.

*c. Visualizing Your Ideal Future:* **Use** visualization techniques to imagine your ideal future. Create a vivid picture in your mind of what you want to achieve, experience, or become. This helps clarify your goals and increases motivation.

*2. Setting Specific and Measurable Goals:*

*a. Clarity and Specificity*: **Clearly define** your goals and make them specific. Instead of vague aspirations, create well-defined objectives that are measurable and achievable.

*b. Break It Down*: **Break** your goals into smaller, manageable steps. This makes them more attainable and allows you to track your progress along the way.

*c. SMART Goals:* **Apply** the SMART goal-setting framework. Ensure that your goals are Specific, Measurable, Achievable, Relevant, and Time-bound. This provides a clear roadmap for success.

### 3. Writing Your Intentions:

*a. Putting It on Paper:* **Write down your intentions and goals. This act of writing helps solidify them in your mind and brings a sense of commitment and accountability.**

*b. Positive Language:* **Frame your intentions in positive language. Instead of focusing on what you want to avoid or change, emphasize what you want to create or manifest in your life.**

*c. Affirmations:* **Create affirmations that support your goals and desires. Use positive statements that reinforce your belief in your ability to achieve them. Repeat these affirmations regularly to strengthen your intention.**

### 4. Taking Aligned Action:

*a. Action Plan:* **Create** a detailed action plan that outlines the steps you need to take to achieve your goals. Break them down into actionable tasks and set deadlines for each.

*b. Consistency and Commitment:* **Commit** to taking consistent action towards your goals. Stay motivated and dedicated, even when faced with challenges or setbacks.

*c. Course Correction:* **Regularly** assess your progress and make adjustments as needed. Be open to adapting your plans if necessary while staying aligned with your overall intentions.

Let's consider the story of Mark, who wanted to start his own business. Mark set a powerful intention by clarifying his goals and desires. He visualized his ideal future as a successful entrepreneur and wrote down his intentions and SMART goals. Mark then took aligned action by creating a detailed business plan, networking with industry professionals, and acquiring the necessary skills and resources. Through consistent effort and a clear intention, Mark successfully launched his business and achieved his goal.

Setting powerful intentions clarifies your goals and desires, providing you with focus and direction. By reflecting on your desires, setting specific and measurable goals, writing your intentions, and taking aligned action, you create a roadmap for success. Stay committed, consistent, and open to making adjustments along the way. Remember, your intentions have the power to shape your reality. With clarity and determination, you can manifest your goals and desires in a powerful and meaningful way.

*Strength isn't found in the absence of fear, but in the courage to face it head-on*

# 14. Overcoming Obstacles: Building Resilience and Perseverance

*1. Embracing a Growth Mindset:*

*a. Shifting Perspectives:* **Adopt a growth mindset,** which sees challenges as opportunities for growth and learning. Embrace the belief that you can develop your abilities and overcome obstacles with effort and perseverance.

*b. Reframing Failure:* **View failure as a stepping stone to success rather than a reflection of your worth. See it as an opportunity to learn, adjust your approach, and grow stronger.

*c. Positive Self-Talk:* **Practice positive self-talk and affirmations to cultivate a resilient mindset. Replace negative thoughts with empowering and encouraging statements that reinforce your ability to overcome obstacles.

## 2. Developing Resilience:

*a. Cultivating Self-Awareness:* **Develop** self-awareness to recognize your emotions, thoughts, and reactions to challenges. This allows you to respond effectively and adapt when faced with obstacles.

*b. Building Support Systems:* **Surround** yourself with a supportive network of friends, family, mentors, or a community that can provide encouragement, guidance, and perspective during difficult times.

*c. Self-Care and Stress Management:* **Prioritize** self-care practices to manage stress and maintain your well-being. Engage in activities that recharge and rejuvenate you, such as exercise, mindfulness, hobbies, and spending time in nature.

*3. Perseverance and Determination:*

*a. Goal Orientation:* **Stay focused on your goals and maintain a clear vision of what you want to achieve. Use your goals as motivation to persevere through challenges and setbacks.**

*b. Break It Down:* **Break down big challenges into smaller, manageable steps. This makes them less overwhelming and allows you to make progress, even if it's incremental.**

*c. Celebrate Milestones:* **Acknowledge and celebrate your achievements along the way. Recognize and appreciate the progress you've made, no matter how small. This boosts motivation and reinforces your ability to overcome obstacles.**

## 4. Learning from Setbacks:

*a. Analyzing Lessons:* **When faced with obstacles or setbacks, take time to reflect and analyze the situation. Identify the lessons and insights gained from the experience. Use this knowledge to adjust your approach and improve future outcomes.**

*b. Adaptability and Flexibility:* **Be open to adapting your strategies and approaches as needed. Embrace change and adjust your plans when circumstances require it. This allows you to navigate obstacles with resilience and creativity.**

*c. Persistence:* **Persevere through challenges and maintain a long-term perspective. Understand that success often comes with persistence and the willingness to keep trying even when faced with difficulties.**

Let's consider the story of Sarah, who dreamed of becoming a professional musician. Along her journey, Sarah faced numerous obstacles, including rejections, self-doubt, and setbacks. However, she cultivated a growth mindset and resilience. Sarah sought support from a mentor, practiced consistently, and continued to refine her skills. Despite the challenges, Sarah persevered and eventually achieved her dream, becoming a successful musician. Her ability to overcome obstacles and her unwavering determination led to her success.

Overcoming obstacles requires building resilience and developing a mindset that embraces challenges as opportunities for growth. By cultivating a growth mindset, developing resilience, maintaining perseverance, and learning from setbacks, you can navigate obstacles with strength and determination. Remember, obstacles are a natural part of life, and your ability to overcome them strengthens your character and paves the way for personal growth and success.

*Surround yourself with a supportive network of friends, family, mentors, or a community*

# 15. Achieving True Fulfillment: Taking Aligned Action and Living with Purpose

*1. Clarifying Your Values and Passions:*

*a. Self-Reflection:* **Take time to reflect on your core values and what truly matters to you. Identify the activities, causes, or areas of interest that ignite your passion and bring you a sense of fulfillment.**

*b. Aligning with Your Values:* **Ensure that your actions and decisions align with your values. Living in alignment with your core values brings a deep sense of fulfillment and purpose.**

*c. Exploring Your Passions:* **Engage in activities that energize and inspire you. Experiment with different hobbies, interests, and experiences to discover what resonates with you and brings you joy.**

## 2. Setting Meaningful Goals:

*a. Purposeful Goal-Setting:* **Set goals that align with your values and passions. Define what success means to you based on your own aspirations and desires, rather than external expectations.**

*b. Long-Term Vision:* **Create a clear vision of the life you want to live and the impact you want to make. Set goals that contribute to that vision and provide a sense of purpose and direction.**

*c. Actionable Steps:* **Break down your goals into actionable steps and create a plan to achieve them. Take consistent, focused action towards your goals, celebrating milestones along the way.**

### 3. Taking Aligned Action:

*a. Authenticity and Integrity:* **Live** in alignment with your true self and be true to your values. Make choices and take actions that are congruent with who you are and what you believe in.

*b. Overcoming Fear and Resistance:* **Recognize** that fear and resistance are natural when pursuing meaningful goals. Embrace discomfort and push through limiting beliefs and self-doubt. Take courageous steps towards your aspirations.

*c. Embracing Growth and Learning:* **View** challenges and setbacks as opportunities for growth and learning. Embrace a mindset of continuous improvement and see every experience as a chance to develop new skills and insights.

### 4. Cultivating Mindfulness and Gratitude:

*a. Being Present:* **Practice mindfulness to stay fully present in the current moment. Cultivate awareness and appreciation for the experiences, people, and opportunities that enrich your life.**

*b. Gratitude Practice:* **Cultivate a regular gratitude practice. Reflect on and express gratitude for the things you have, the people in your life, and the progress you've made. This fosters a positive mindset and enhances your sense of fulfillment.**

*c. Celebration and Reflection:* **Take time to celebrate your achievements and milestones. Reflect on the progress you've made and acknowledge the impact of your actions. This reinforces your sense of purpose and fulfillment.**

Let's consider the story of Alex, who felt unfulfilled in their corporate job. Alex embarked on a journey to discover their true passions and values. Through self-reflection, Alex realized their passion for environmental sustainability. They set a meaningful goal to start a business that promotes sustainable products. Alex took aligned action by acquiring the necessary knowledge, creating a business plan, and launching their venture. By living in alignment with their values and passions, Alex found true fulfillment and a deep sense of purpose.

Achieving true fulfillment requires taking aligned action and living with purpose. Clarify your values and passions, set meaningful goals, and take consistent action towards them. Embrace authenticity, overcome fear and resistance, and cultivate a growth mindset. Practice mindfulness and gratitude to stay present and appreciative of your journey. Remember, true fulfillment comes from living a life that aligns with your values, passions, and aspirations, making a positive impact, and embracing growth along the way.

*Reflect on and express gratitude for the things you have, the people in your life, and the progress you've made.*

# Conclusion:

## Embodying Your Worthiness Transformation

Embarking on a journey of embodying your worthiness transformation is a powerful and transformative process. Throughout this journey, you have explored various aspects of personal growth, including setting powerful intentions, overcoming obstacles, building resilience, living with purpose, and taking aligned action. By integrating these principles into your life, you can experience a profound shift in how you perceive yourself and your place in the world.

Recognizing and embracing your inherent worthiness is a fundamental step in this transformation. You have learned that your worthiness is not contingent upon external validation or achievements but is an innate aspect of your being. As you cultivate self-acceptance and self-love, you create a strong foundation for personal growth and fulfillment.

Setting powerful intentions clarifies your goals and desires, providing you with focus and direction. By clarifying your values, passions, and long-term vision, you have discovered what truly brings you fulfillment and purpose. Through the process of setting meaningful goals and taking aligned action, you have learned to overcome obstacles, cultivate resilience, and persevere in the face of challenges.

Throughout this journey, you have developed a growth mindset, embracing the belief that challenges are opportunities for growth and learning. By reframing failure, adapting to change, and persisting in the pursuit of your goals, you have demonstrated resilience and determination.

Mindfulness and gratitude have become integral practices in your life, allowing you to stay present, appreciate the journey, and celebrate your achievements. These practices deepen your connection with yourself, others, and the world around you, fostering a sense of interconnectedness and abundance.

As you embody your worthiness transformation, you radiate confidence, authenticity, and a deep sense of purpose. Your transformation serves as an inspiration to those around you, empowering them to embark on their own journeys of self-discovery and growth.

Remember, this transformation is an ongoing process, and it requires commitment, self-compassion, and continued self-reflection. Embrace the journey with an open heart and mind, knowing that true fulfillment lies in living a life aligned with your values, passions, and aspirations.

You are worthy of all the love, joy, and success that life has to offer. Embody your worthiness, embrace your transformation, and continue to shine your light brightly in the world.

# Review

Dear Reader

I hope this message finds you well. As the author of **Embrace Your Worthiness**, I am reaching out to express my sincere gratitude for choosing to embark on this journey of personal transformation

Your insights are invaluable, and I would love to hear your thoughts on this book. Whether it's a brief comment or a more detailed review, your feedback contributes to the ongoing dialogue around **Embrace Your Worthiness**

What resonated with you the most in the book?
Were there specific tools or insights that you found particularly helpful?

How has this book influenced your approach to personal transformation?

Your honest feedback not only helps me as an author but also provides potential readers with valuable insights. If you could take a minute to share your thoughts on [platforms where the book is available, e.g., Amazon], it would mean a great deal.

Thank you for being part of this journey. Your voice matters and I appreciate your time and consideration.

Wishing you continued growth and the best,
Dr. Sherrie R. Salls, PhD
Author, Embrace Your Worthiness.

www.ingramcontent.com/pod-product-compliance
Lightning Source LLC
Chambersburg PA
CBHW050315230526
45471CB00005B/2195